CLASSICAL GIANTS

Beethoven

Classical Giants: Beethoven

1st Edition published 2023.

First published by Calendar House Press 2023

www.classicalgiants.com

Cover design by Luneview Publishing

Illustrations by Evgenia Lanskikh

Designed and Typeset by Calendar House Press

Classical Giants series vol.1: Beethoven

ISBN: 978-1-916687-00-4

What people have to say about Classical Giants:

★★★★★ **A treasure trove for inquisitive minds**

This volume paints a vivid portrait of George Frideric Handel, intertwining his masterpieces with the story of his life. It's a compelling read.

Mrs. N. Davis, Amazon

★★★★★ **A wonderful peek into the world of Handel!**

This is the second book in this series that I've read, and I'm so impressed by the quality and readability of these amazing little books. I learn so much more in my time reading these books than I have in the other 39 years of soaking up random tidbits of musical history. I recommend for anyone!

Juanita, Amazon

★★★★★ **Inspired!**

Wow- reading this, I became quite fond of Handel, and he would definitely be on my list for the ultimate dinner party guest! Full of facts and information delivered with humour, delightful illustrations, and a captivating style, "A musical handshake across time" - just perfect!

Katie Hockey, Amazon

★★★★★ **Unknown Handel historical facts**

Such interesting facts. I had no idea about so much of this composer's life. This book enlightens you and gives a feel of what life was like back then.

L Snowdon, Amazon

★★★★★ **A masterpiece quick read**

The author, Emma Warner-Reed, did an amazing job describing some very interesting facts about the GREAT BEAR. You can really see the passion in the pages that describe the greatness, changes, and uniqueness (size and temper, in this case) of these Great Classical Giants. I had no idea that a resource like this was so freely available. Excellent read, highly recommend.

JMA, Amazon

★★★★★ **What a great idea for a series**

This is such a great idea. As a parent, I learned so much in just a short well-written book. It's easily something kids can enjoy, especially those interested in history, music and period pieces. Looking forward to the next ones to read with my kids.

Ole K Birkeland, Amazon

★★★★★ **I never knew that about Beethoven!**

This was such an enjoyable read! The interesting facts are the hero of the story through which Ludwig Beethoven absolutely springs to life. Emma Warner-Reed writes with a style that is relatable and brimming with simple comparisons to life today that made me feel as though I was reading about someone's great-uncle in a not-so-distant past. Humorous hand-drawn illustrations in the style of Quentin Blake...complement the book perfectly - causing me to laugh out loud often.

Tigg, Amazon

★★★★★ **A Journey Through Music: Tchaikovsky's Life for Children**

A delightful and insightful addition to the world of children's literature, especially for those with a keen interest in music history. Crafted with passion and a deep understanding of the need for accessible music history resources for children, this book stands out for its engaging narrative and stunning illustrations that bring the story of Pyotr Ilyich Tchaikovsky to life. The author, drawing from personal experience and a desire to share the richness of classical music with young minds, introduces Tchaikovsky not just as a distant figure in history but as a real person with relatable emotions and experiences.

What sets this book apart is its ability to make classical music history accessible and engaging to a younger audience, fostering an early appreciation for the arts. It is a commendable effort to fill a gap in children's literature, making "Classical Giants: Tchaikovsky" a must-read for musical families and anyone looking to introduce children to the wonders of classical music and the stories of those who created it.

Chris S, Amazon

Classical Giants: the purpose of the series

The idea behind this series is to bring to life the most famous composers in history for children: not simply as a list of dates and ordered 'works,' but as actual characters who lived and breathed on an accurate historical timeline.

In taking this more holistic approach to learning, we at Calendar House Press hope to create for young readers a window into the life of classical composers, showing them not only what the composers were like as people but also what made them tick: what happened around them during their lifetimes, what was important to them, what influenced them and what inspired them to create their greatest masterpieces.

We hope you enjoy this introduction to the real life of the first of our Classical Giants: Beethoven.

How to use this book

For children, the intention is simply for them to read the book, consume the knowledge, and enjoy it!

For teachers and home educators, *Beethoven*, from the Classical Giants series, is:

- an interesting non-fiction title for the reading corner or library shelves
- a comprehensive music history sourcebook for children in years 3 and beyond
- a springboard into a series of linked reference topics, taking children on a lesson of discovery through the mediums of:

  - ✓ Art
  - ✓ Humanities
  - ✓ Mathematics
  - ✓ PSHE
  - ✓ English
  - ✓ Science
  - ✓ Religious Education

For further information and ideas on using this book in the classroom, visit the website at **www.classicalgiants.com**.

A word about classical music

The term 'classical music' can mean two different things. First, it is a general term that refers to Western music played by an orchestra or orchestral instruments. It uses a particular musical form, such as a symphony, a concerto, or a string quartet.

But the term 'classical' also refers to a particular period in music history, beginning in 1750 - just before the birth of Mozart (in 1756) and ending in 1830 - just after the death of Beethoven (in 1827). The Classical period is considered the most critical period in orchestral music because it is when musical forms such as the symphony, the concerto, and the sonata were perfected.

There are six recognised periods of classical music:

- **Pre-1400** **Medieval**
- **1400 to 1600** **Renaissance**
- **1600 to 1750** **Baroque**
- **1750 to 1830** **Classical**
- **1830 to 1900** **Romantic**
- **1900 onwards** **20th/ 21st Centuries**

Beethoven lived during the **Classical** period.

Table of contents

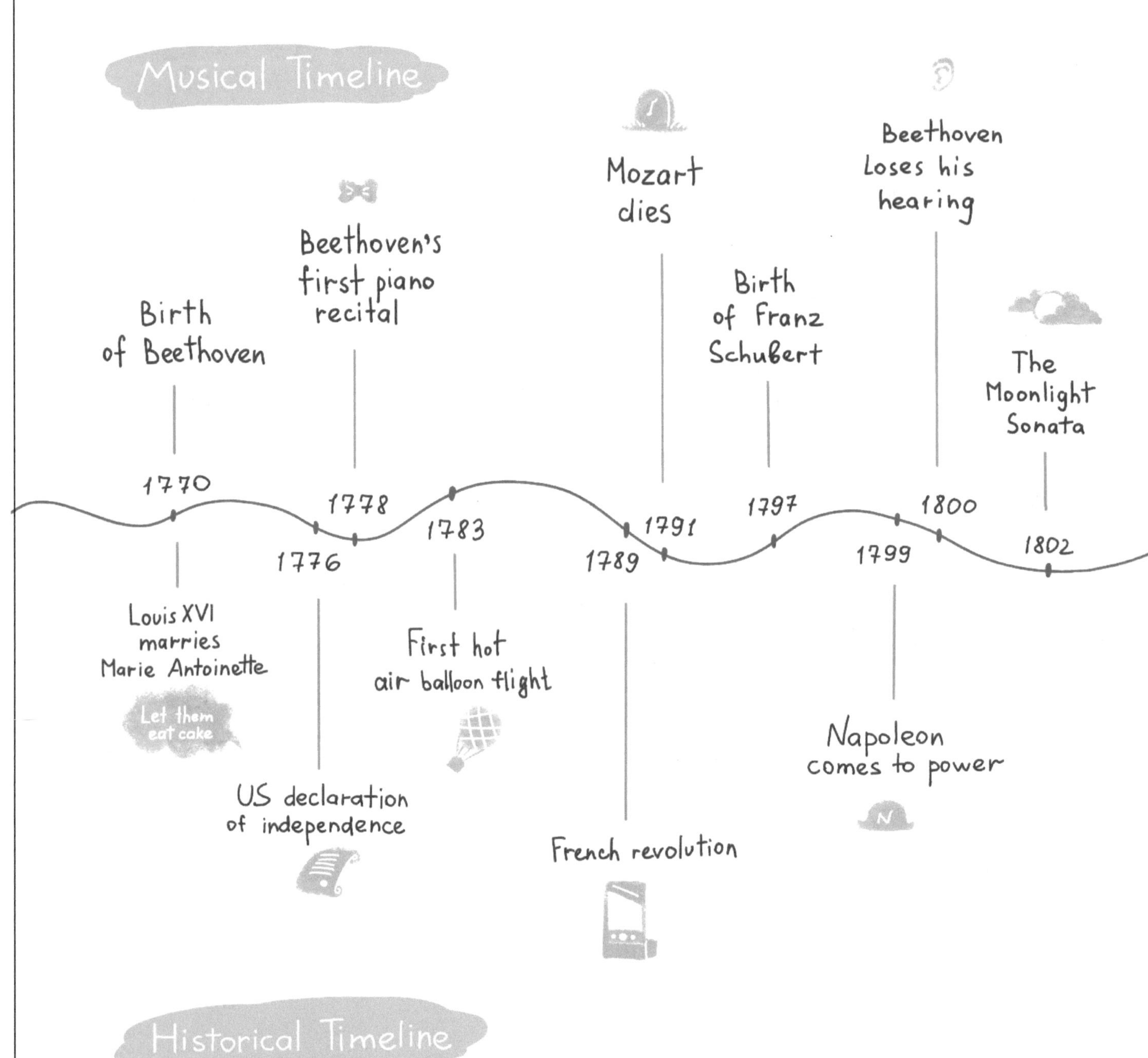
Musical Timeline
Birth of Beethoven
1770
Beethoven's first piano recital
1778
Mozart dies
1791
Birth of Franz Schubert
1797
Beethoven Loses his hearing
1800
The Moonlight Sonata
1802
1776
1783
1789
1799
Louis XVI marries Marie Antoinette
Let them eat cake
US declaration of independence
First hot air balloon flight
French revolution
Napoleon comes to power
N
Historical Timeline

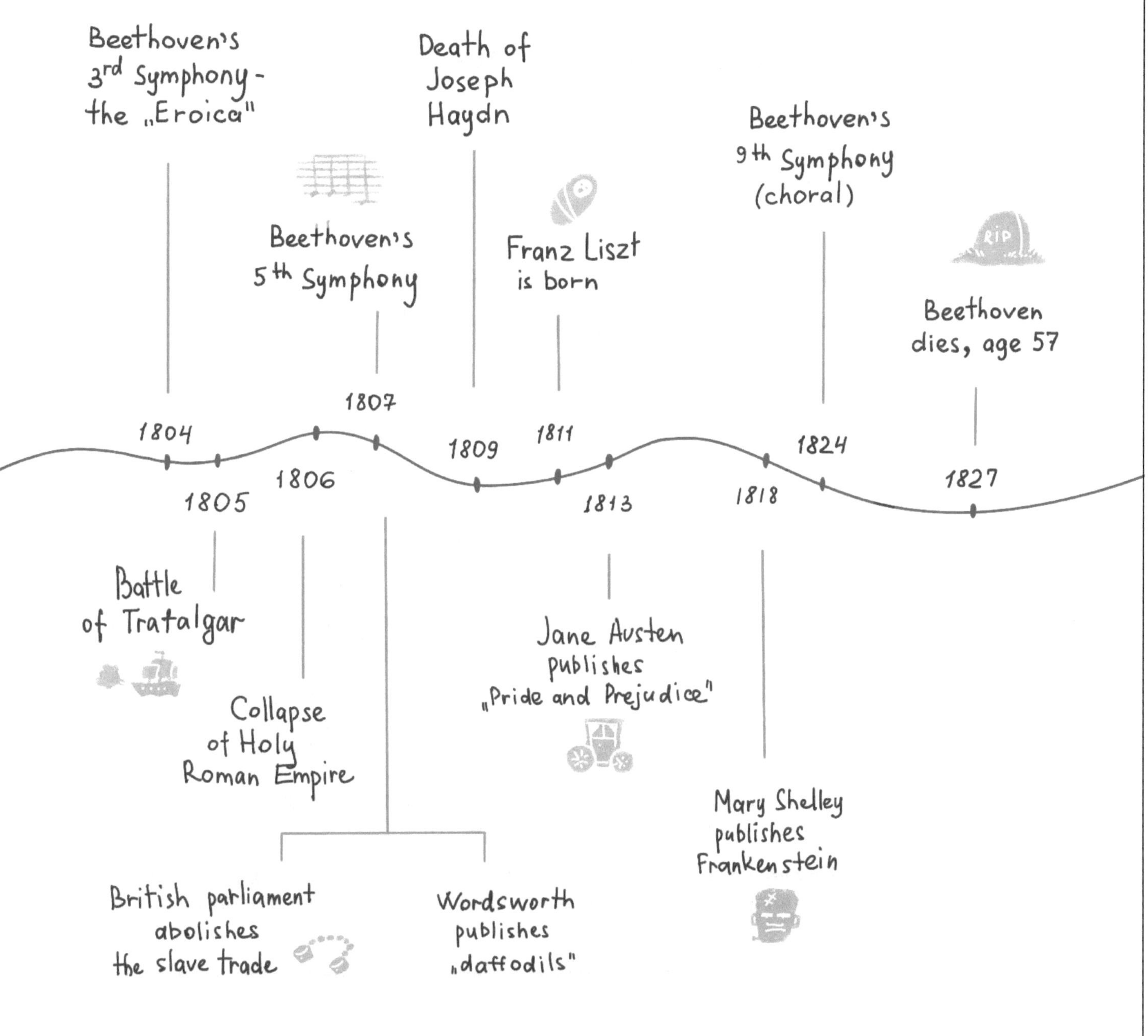
Beethoven's 3rd Symphony - the „Eroica"
1804
1805
Battle of Trafalgar
1806
Collapse of Holy Roman Empire
Beethoven's 5th Symphony
1807
British parliament abolishes the slave trade
Wordsworth publishes „daffodils"
Death of Joseph Haydn
1809
Franz Liszt is born
1811
1813
Jane Austen publishes „Pride and Prejudice"
1818
Mary Shelley publishes Frankenstein
Beethoven's 9th Symphony (choral)
1824
RIP
Beethoven dies, age 57
1827

1. Where was Beethoven born?

Ludwig van Beethoven was born around 15th December 1770 in the Holy Roman Empire in a small town called Bonn. We don't know Beethoven's exact date of birth as he has no surviving birth certificate. But we do know that he was Christened on 17th December 1770, making it reasonably certain that he would have been born a day or two beforehand. In those days, it was the custom to christen babies quickly after birth.

Perhaps more importantly, we also know that Beethoven himself celebrated his birthday on the 15th, and if it's good enough for him, it is good enough for us!

The Holy Roman Empire

During Beethoven's lifetime, Germany didn't exist, as such. The area where he lived was part of a large group of member states known as the Holy Roman Empire.

Although it was called an empire, it wasn't what we imagine an empire to be today. It wasn't one big country ruling over others. Instead, it was a bunch of smaller countries working together in agreement, a bit like the modern European Union.

Some of the countries included in the Empire were Germany, Austria, and parts of Italy. All the countries in the Empire were Catholic.

The Holy Roman Empire was formed way back in the year 800 and lasted for many, many years, right up until the early 1800s. So, you can imagine it was around for a really long time.

"Quick – to the church with him!"

Beethoven was the eldest of three brothers. His younger brother, Kaspar, was born in 1774, and the youngest, Nikolaus, was born in 1776. Beethoven's parents had another boy before him, also called Ludwig, but he died at only six days old. Happily, the Ludwig van Beethoven we know survived.

2. What kind of world was Beethoven born into?

Beethoven was born in the 'Age of Enlightenment,' which sounds rather wonderful, doesn't it? During this time, people began opening their eyes to new ideas and learning, art and literature. Writers and artists started to create in a free and less formulaic pattern than before, using their work to portray the beauty that could be found in the force and unpredictability of nature. It was a time of great experimentation and growth and a particularly exciting place in history to be for a musician like Beethoven.

Social and political thinking was also advancing at this time; consequently, there was a great deal of political unrest in Europe. The town of Bonn, where Beethoven was born, and the city of Vienna in Austria, where he spent most of his adulthood while Beethoven was growing up, formed part of the Holy Roman Empire. The Empire had once spanned central Europe, but it had been in decline for some years, and people were looking for change.

For those living in the dwindling empire, revolution and revolt seemed to be all around them. As a young man in his teens, Beethoven followed news of the political unrest in France and, at 19, watched as the leaders of the **French Revolution** crushed their country's monarchy. Beethoven was also to see the fall of the Holy Roman Empire itself during his lifetime.

The French Revolution

The French Revolution was a big turning point in history when the people of France got rid of the French Monarchy (the king and queen), and France became a republic, which means the people had more say in how things were run.

Before the revolution started, there was a lot of trouble in France. People were unhappy with the way things were and wanted change. Then, on 14 July 1789, something important happened. A group of people stormed the Bastille, which was a big old fortress and prison. This event is considered the official start of the revolution.

After that, things got even more intense. The French people didn't want a king anymore, and they executed their king, Louis XVI, in January 1793. But the story didn't end there. After the king's execution, the government wanted to get rid of anyone who supported the old king or the rich people of France. This was a time called 'the Reign of Terror.' It was a very scary time for the people of France when many people were put to death.

Beethoven believed strongly in the ideals that guided France's revolution and in its motto: *'liberté, égalité, fraternité,'* which meant 'freedom, equality, and brotherhood.' He believed that all people were created equal and that how much money they had and their importance should be based on how hard they worked and how good they were at their job, not just the family they were born into.

He was also a great admirer of Napoleon Bonaparte, an influential military leader who came to power immediately after the revolution and became the first leader of liberated France.

Beethoven even dedicated his third **symphony** (the Eroica, or 'heroic' symphony) to Bonaparte in honour of his heroism in the name of the ordinary people.

However, Beethoven did not remain a fan of Napoleon for long. When Napoleon crowned himself Emperor of France, Beethoven saw this as a betrayal of his belief that no one is worth more than anyone else and turned against him. Beethoven was so angry with his former idol that he scratched Bonaparte's name off his Eroica symphony with enough force to make a hole in the paper!

"Damn you, Bonaparte!"

3. What was life at home like for Beethoven?

Beethoven's family was a musical one: his father and grandfather were musicians working in the court of the Elector of Cologne (the elector was the name given to heads of state within the Holy Roman Empire). As a singer in the court, Beethoven's father didn't make much money. However, he earned a little more by working as a music tutor to courtiers' children. When Beethoven was first born, Beethoven's Grandfather helped out wherever he could. But the older man died when Beethoven was only three, leaving the family's fortunes in the hands of Beethoven's father.

Beethoven's mother was kind and gentle, as his grandfather had been, but his father was not very loving or kind to him. He recognized his son's talent, but only as a way of making money. He had seen how famous the six-year-old **child prodigy** Wolfgang Amadeus Mozart had become only 15 years earlier, and he dreamed of the same for Beethoven. He began to teach Beethoven both violin and piano at the age of only three. His father was an impatient teacher, making him practice for hours and sometimes even getting him up during the night to practice the piano.

In March 1778, when Beethoven was only seven years old, his father arranged for him to play his first public concert in the city of Cologne. Although young Beethoven was a year older, his father advertised that he was only six, hoping the public would recognise Beethoven as a child prodigy, as Mozart had been before him.

People came from far and wide to hear Beethoven perform, but although he was exceptionally good for his age, the public did not honour Beethoven with the title of 'child genius' as they had Mozart.

Beethoven's father did not take the news well, and things might have been worse for Beethoven was it not for a new court organist hired by the Elector of Cologne to play at that time. Hearing Beethoven's playing, the organist, a man called Christian Neefe, decided to take the young Ludwig under his wing and asked Beethoven's father if he might give the child lessons.

Luckily, Beethoven's father agreed, and things went so well with Neefe that, by the time Beethoven was twelve, Neefe was confident to leave his student in charge of the court **orchestra** when he went away on business!

Given his early experience at the hands of his father, it is surprising that Beethoven had any desire to continue playing. But he loved music and kept on performing and composing for the rest of his life.

'Rubbish!'

4. What was Beethoven like?

Perhaps because his father pushed him so hard from an early age, Beethoven believed music was everything and that how he looked to others was unnecessary. As a result, he was scruffy at best, with unruly hair and dirty, and often torn, clothes. His manners could have been better, and he largely ignored the social niceties of the time. He could be charming to those he liked and rude to those he didn't!

He was bullied by the other children at school, who didn't understand him, but this did not make Beethoven change his ways. Instead, it made him even more determined to become a great **composer** and prove that looks were unrelated to genius. In any case, he had no time for school friends, as he was far too busy practising the piano.

As a grown man, he was short and stocky, standing only 165 centimetres tall, with wild dark hair and eyes and a booming voice that could knock you over at twenty paces. He was so wrapped up in his music that he often forgot to wash or to bother in the least about his surroundings or the way he dressed. Once old enough to rent his own apartment, it was as dirty and messy as him.

Nor did Beethoven look after his instruments. He was constantly breaking his piano and having to send for another. Pianos were a lot less sturdy in his day. The design for the modern piano, with its strong metal frame, was only launched in 1825, two years before Beethoven's death. Before that, pianos were lighter and much easier to damage.

"Look - it's that weirdo Beethoven. Cross the road before he sees us!"

Beethoven's manners did not improve with age, either. He was short-tempered and unpredictable and was often in trouble for being unfriendly to people. While out and about in the town, he tended to mutter to himself and was forever whipping out his notebook to scribble down a fragment of music or an idea. People found this strange and so managed to avoid him if they could.

Despite all this, Beethoven also had a softer side. He loved nature and the outdoors and liked to spend time in the countryside. His 6th symphony, the *Pastoral*, is devoted to his love of nature.

Symphony No.6 (the Pastoral), first movement

Beethoven's handwriting was messy, too, and printers had great difficulty understanding it. Beethoven's brother, Kaspar, often copied out musical **scores** for him so that they could be more easily read. Sadly, Kaspar, who also wrote his own music, took advantage of his position, selling his own **composition**s to the printers and pretending his famous brother had written them. He then kept the money for himself. When Beethoven found out his brother was doing this, it caused them to fall out.

Social and Class Distinctions in the 18th Century

In the 1700s a person's position in life was dictated, not by their talents or achievements, but by their social status, or class. There was a very clear system of social ranking, with the poor working classes at the bottom and the land-owning aristocrats at the top, and a person's place on this ladder governed everything about their life.

The one way to move up the social ladder was to own land. Landowners held power and influence. But, even back then, land was expensive and considered a luxury for the very wealthy.

A poor person might spend their whole life trying to move up the social ladder and gain some form of wealth and "class," but, like Beethoven, if they got anywhere, they would most likely be ridiculed and pitied for their lack of social graces.

The education system was in part to blame for this. The wealthy were able to send their children to school, something which was out of reach of an ordinary man at this time.

5. Did Beethoven marry or have children?

Beethoven never found love, although he kept hoping for it. According to a close friend of Beethoven's, Franz Wegeler, "Beethoven was always in love with someone."

For one reason or another, it never ended happily. Whenever poor Beethoven fell in love, the girl of his dreams would either be already married or not a social match for him. We know of several of their names:

Magdalena Willmann

An **opera** singer whom Beethoven asked to marry him in 1795. She said no, agreeing to marry a wealthy merchant only a year later.

Countess Giulietta Guicciardi

The countess began taking piano lessons from Beethoven when she was 17, and Beethoven fell head-over-heels in love with her. He composed one of his most famous pieces of piano music for her: the *Moonlight* ***Sonata***. Sadly, he was not her social equal. She later married a Count and moved to Italy. Beethoven kept a portrait of her in his desk drawer until he died.

She loves him, not...

Countess Josephine Deym

Again, the Countess was not a social match for Beethoven. The countess was a young widow, and marrying Beethoven would have affected her children's social status, so she ended their relationship.

Countess Therese von Brunswick

The same happened here, too. Poor Beethoven!

Amalie Sebald

She was a singer who nursed Beethoven through an illness, winning his heart. However, they ended up being just good friends.

Therese Malfatti

The eighteen-year-old daughter of Beethoven's doctor was the last love of Beethoven that we know about. The girl's family disapproved, mainly because Beethoven was forty by this time. Beethoven's famous piano piece 'Für Elise' is believed by some to be dedicated to this, his final love. Beethoven never tried to find love again.

Excerpt from *Für Elise*

Beethoven did not have children of his own. But, after his brother Kaspar died of tuberculosis, he was named guardian of Kaspar's 9-year-old son, Karl, together with the boy's mother. Unfortunately, Beethoven and his sister-in-law hated each other and fought constantly for custody of the child.

"He's mine!"... "No, he's mine!"

Beethoven eventually won this battle, although close friends suggested he wasn't the best father, something which Beethoven himself admitted, with regret, when he realised later on in the boy's life how heartbroken the feud between Beethoven and his mother had made Karl.

6. Is it true that Beethoven was deaf?

One of the greatest tragedies of Beethoven's life was that he went deaf at an early age. He started having difficulty hearing while still in his twenties, and this got steadily worse until, by the time Beethoven was 45, he had lost his hearing altogether.

To begin with, he tried to hide his deafness, afraid that people would believe that if he could not hear music, he would no longer be able to compose or perform. Being deaf didn't stop Beethoven from hearing the music in his head, though; much of his work was written after he had completely lost his hearing.

Excerpt from *Moonlight Sonata*

By the time he was thirty, Beethoven was forced to admit he was struggling to hear, after which he began carrying an ear trumpet to help him hear better.

The thing Beethoven found most frustrating about his deafness was that it affected his ability to communicate effectively with other people. Because of his loss of hearing, he was often misinterpreted and is frequently remembered as a grumpy, unsociable man. In truth, however, he was a very social animal and hated his inability to connect with others.

As his hearing worsened, Beethoven became more and more reclusive until he disappeared from public life altogether. He did use conversation books, though – simple notebooks that he used to converse with his closest friends when they visited him. They would write what they wanted to say, and he would answer by speaking to them, often quite loudly! Over 400 of these little books were found in his rooms after his death.

No one could discover what caused Beethoven's deafness or other health conditions. Beethoven, during his lifetime, went to see many different doctors, but none could give him an answer. Beethoven asked for his body to be examined after his death to see if the cause could be found. The doctors found that the nerves in his ears through which sound travelled were damaged, but they could not find anything to tell them how this had happened.

One theory that has come to light much more recently is that Beethoven may have suffered from lead poisoning. By inspecting hair and skull fragments, researchers found high levels of lead in Beethoven's body. As people weren't aware of lead poisoning or its effects during Beethoven's lifetime, this is entirely possible: Beethoven would have been regularly exposed to lead, even eating and drinking from lead cups and plates.

7. Who were Beethoven's musical contemporaries?

A contemporary is somebody who is alive at the same time as you. Here are some of Beethoven's musical contemporaries:

- **Joseph Haydn 1732-1809**

  Haydn was known as the 'father of the symphony.' He was a prolific composer, and by the time he and Beethoven met, he had already composed over 100 symphonies. Beethoven became a student of Haydn's for a year, but Haydn found Beethoven challenging to teach. Although the two often clashed, Beethoven respected Haydn, and they remained in touch until Haydn's death.

- **Wolfgang Amadeus Mozart 1756-1791**

  Mozart was 14 years Beethoven's senior and already an established composer when Beethoven met him. Beethoven would have known about Mozart from early childhood, mainly because Beethoven's father wanted him to be like Mozart and follow in his success as a child prodigy. Beethoven performed for Mozart once during his first visit to Vienna in 1787. He hoped to impress Mozart enough that he would offer to teach Beethoven, but this never happened. By the time Beethoven returned to Vienna in 1792, Mozart had died.

- **Franz Schubert 1797-1828**

  It is not thought that the two men ever met in person, but Schubert was a big fan. Schubert said that he once saw Beethoven across a crowded coffee house but was too star-struck to go over to talk to him. Scores of Schubert's songs were brought to Beethoven's deathbed, and the composer announced that he was impressed, which must have made Schubert very proud. When Schubert died only a year later, he asked to be buried in a grave next to Beethoven's. The two remain together to this day.

- **Franz Liszt 1811-1886**

  Liszt met Beethoven in 1823, four years before Beethoven's death, at Beethoven's house in Vienna. After playing one of Beethoven's piano **concerto**s, Beethoven approached Liszt, taking him by both hands and kissing him on the forehead. Liszt remembered their meeting for the rest of his life and described it as his proudest moment.

at last...
Beethoven
SCHUBERT

8. Did Beethoven meet his contemporaries?

As we have seen above, yes, he did!

Beethoven and Mozart

One of Beethoven's musical heroes was Wolfgang Amadeus Mozart. He had hoped Mozart might take him under his wing and agree to become Beethoven's teacher, but sadly, this never happened.

In 1787 Beethoven's teacher, Neefe, asked the Elector if he could take Beethoven to Vienna and arrange an introduction to Mozart. The Elector agreed and said that he would fund the trip. At this time, Vienna was the unofficial capital of the Holy Roman Empire and the Empire's musical capital, so this was very exciting for Beethoven.

On listening to the 17-year-old Beethoven play the piano, to Beethoven's disappointment, Mozart didn't seem impressed. However, when he later heard Beethoven's improvising, which was a natural skill of Beethoven's, Mozart was heard to say:

'Keep your eyes on him; someday, he will give the world something to talk about.'

Beethoven was keen to set up another meeting so that he could impress Mozart some more.

But unfortunately, Beethoven never got the opportunity, as he was called back to Bonn. His mother was sick, and he was needed to help nurse her through her illness.

Beethoven's mother died a month after his return home, leaving Beethoven alone to care for his ill-tempered and, by this time, unwell father and his two younger brothers. This was a difficult time for Beethoven as he was put under a great deal of financial and emotional strain. He had to earn money to clothe and feed himself and his brothers, playing the viola in the court orchestra in Bonn and giving piano lessons, so he had little opportunity to write.

It was four years before Beethoven was able to return to Vienna. By this time, Mozart had died.

Beethoven and Haydn

Beethoven did manage to catch the attention of a friend of Mozart's and another of Beethoven's musical contemporaries, Joseph Haydn. While passing through Bonn, Haydn was handed a copy of one of Beethoven's compositions, a ***Cantata*** *on the Death of the Emperor*. Haydn was so impressed that he asked Beethoven to return to Vienna with Haydn as his pupil.

Beethoven and Haydn didn't get on terribly well. Haydn was, by then, an older man and old-fashioned in his outlook and struggled to accept Beethoven's brutish behaviour. He felt

Beethoven should try to look clean and tidy as a mark of respect for his teacher and that he should respect Haydn's superior knowledge of the musical conventions that existed at that time.

Beethoven did not want to follow the strict rules of composition used by those who had gone before him. He preferred to learn through trial and error, expanding and bending the rules to make his own kind of music.

Symphony No.5

About a year after becoming Beethoven's teacher, Haydn left Vienna to go to London, England. Despite their differences, Beethoven wanted to remain on good terms with Haydn, and he took him out for coffee and chocolate at a local café.

This simply won't do

9. Did Beethoven have a patron?

Beethoven wasn't a stranger to **patronage** and had several **patrons** during his life. What is different about Beethoven is that he wasn't wholly financially dependent on his patrons. He also made money from hosting public concerts and selling his music for others to play.

The Patronage System

A patron is someone who pays an artist or musician so that they can carry out their work. Much like a sponsor, today.

In those days, music was for the rich. The only people who got to hear or enjoy classical music were those who played it in their grand houses for groups of friends or family.

Musicians worked under the patronage of one or more nobles or aristocrats, living in their courts and composing music at their patrons' whims.

Beethoven's independence from his patrons was a first and was significant, not only because he brought music to the masses (poor people could afford to go to Beethoven's concerts) but also because Beethoven had enough of his own money that he didn't always have to do what his patrons wanted. He could write whatever he chose and explore new expression in music and play with its **form** in a way that had never happened before. This was called creative freedom.

Ludwig,
I have friends
coming over on Saturday.
I wonder if you might
compose a small opus
for us?

Nope,
not in
the
mood

The most notable of Beethoven's patrons were:

Count Ferdinand Ernst Gabriel von Waldstein

Count Ferdinand paid for Beethoven's move to Vienna and gave him essential introductions through the court.

Maximillian Franz, Elector of Cologne

The Elector was the brother of Marie Antoinette, Queen of France. Beethoven played in Franz's orchestra, and Franz introduced Beethoven to Joseph Haydn.

Prince Karl Lichnowsky

The prince allowed Beethoven to live in his palace in Vienna for six years and paid him a generous wage. Sadly, they fell out after Beethoven refused to perform at the court for guests of the prince, who were French officers.

Prince Franz Joseph Maximilian von Lobkowitz

Prince Franz was a friend of Count Ferdinand, who maintained his own orchestra and paid Beethoven a salary for many years before he was bankrupted during the war with France and left Vienna.

10. What music is Beethoven famous for?

Beethoven wrote a great deal for piano and orchestra during his lifetime, and he even wrote an opera. He is perhaps best known for his symphonies, though, of which he wrote nine. Arguably the most famous are his third (the 'Eroica'), fifth (Da-na-na-NAHhhhhh), sixth ('Pastoral'), and ninth symphonies.

Beethoven's third - The Eroica Symphony (Italian for 'heroic')

Beethoven's third symphony was initially written to celebrate the military leader, Napoleon Bonaparte, of whom Beethoven was in awe as a young man. The piece is full of heroic **themes**, but it is most famous for representing Beethoven's move from traditional **classical** composition into a new, enlightened era of music-making.

The Eroica sounds utterly different from everything that had gone before – including Beethoven's own first two symphonies. It is twice as long as anything written before it, too.

Beethoven's Fifth – The Fate Symphony

Beethoven's fifth symphony, sometimes called the 'Fate' symphony (although Beethoven never called it that), has a dramatic, stormy beginning. The composition is unique in that whole of the first **movement** centres around a four-note **phrase** – and three of the four are the same note! How Beethoven creates an entire piece of music by playing around with a simple, four-note phrase shows his cleverness.

The fifth symphony is considered one of the most important works of the classical period. Indeed, it was considered so important that a recording of it was sent into space in 1977 as part of a human time capsule!

Beethoven's Sixth - The Pastoral Symphony

The Pastoral Symphony was dedicated to Beethoven's love of nature and the countryside. The symphony is divided into five sections, or 'movements,' which is unusual because, until Beethoven's time, symphonies were typically split into only four parts.

Each of the five movements of the Pastoral has a name showing what the movement represents. So, the first is the feeling of joy upon arriving in the countryside (Beethoven loved the great outdoors, so this would have been a musical reflection of his feelings when he visited the country).

The second movement depicts a scene by a brook. The third movement depicts peasants feasting and dancing. The fourth represents a thunderstorm, and the final, fifth movement is a shepherd's song after the storm.

If you want to see the Pastoral in action, Disney made a wonderful interpretation of this in their first full-length motion picture, Fantasia.

As well as his symphonies, Beethoven wrote a lot of piano music, some of which he dedicated to the various loves of his life, such as the ***Moonlight Sonata*** and ***Für Elise***.

11. What is unique about Beethoven's 'Tenth'?

Around 1817, the Royal Philharmonic Society in London asked Beethoven to write his ninth and tenth symphonies. Beethoven completed his Ninth Symphony in 1824 and began work on the tenth. But he did not live long enough to complete it. Ever since then, Beethoven fans have wondered what might have been had Beethoven been given the chance to finish his last work. But, as the only remains of Beethoven's work in progress are some musical sketches of the first movement, which he started before his death in 1827, it remained no more than a dream – until now.

In 1988, an expert in musical composition called Barry Cooper tried to recreate the first movement of Beethoven's Tenth Symphony, putting together 250 bars of music from Beethoven's original sketches to produce as faithfully as possible what might have been. Cooper's score was first performed at a concert given in 1988 by the Royal Philharmonic Society, London, who had commissioned the new symphony in 1827. But without any more material to work from, he was unable to complete the remaining movements.

Now, thanks to artificial intelligence technology, Beethoven's vision has finally been brought to life. The project was started in 2019 by a group made up of music historians, musicologists, composers, and computer scientists and took over two years to complete.

But how did they do it? How could these fragments be turned into a complete piece of music? And how could they ensure, while using artificial intelligence, that the work remained faithful to Beethoven's process and vision?

The team used notes and completed compositions from all of Beethoven's works, along with the available sketches from the Tenth Symphony, to create something that they believed Beethoven himself might have written. Some helpful hints in Beethoven's letters told them about his plans for the symphony: for example, they discovered that he had wanted the Tenth Symphony to end with a choral work, like the Ninth. In the end, though, they had to teach a machine not only everything Beethoven had ever written but also how he actually went about making music to put together and orchestrate the remaining movements.

The work premiered in Beethoven's birthplace in Bonn, Germany, 194 years after the composer's death.

Some say that artificial intelligence should not be used to tamper with the creative arts and should be an entirely human process. Others would argue that, while artificial intelligence is not a replacement, it can be used as a tool, opening doors for artists to express themselves in new ways. What do you think?

12. What should Beethoven be remembered for?

Beethoven died at home in bed of pneumonia on March 26th, 1827. He was in his 57th year. His last words were, “It’s a shame, a shame – too late!” Perhaps he was lamenting all the work he never completed. But we think he left a lot to celebrate about! Here are only a few of the reasons why this giant of classical music should be remembered:

- **Beethoven changed the face of music forever**

  By daring to be different and by bringing emotion into his work, he brought the spirit of the Enlightenment to music for the first time.

- **Beethoven brought music to the masses**

  Before him, secular (non-religious) music was reserved only for the wealthy upper classes and the aristocracy.

  Recitals or performances of classical music were held at the homes of the musicians’ wealthy benefactors to the exclusion of the general public. Beethoven changed this by holding public performances for the masses, open to anyone who could afford a ticket.

- **Beethoven made music bigger**!

  He started using orchestras far larger than had been used before. He was the first to use a French horn in an orchestra and the first to use a trombone in an orchestra. He was also the first composer to use a choir in a symphony.

- **Beethoven was the first musician not to rely on his patrons financially**

  By printing and selling his music and doing public performances, Beethoven earned enough to pick and choose his patrons and write the music he wanted to write, rather than being forced to write only what his patrons asked him to produce. He had total creative freedom.

Symphony No.3 (Eroica)

Just from this short book about his life, you will know that Beethoven was both quite an interesting character and a musical genius. What do you think he should be remembered for?

Beethoven
recital

Glossary

$20^{th}/21^{st}$ century	Music written from 1900 onwards
Baroque	The musical period spanning the years between 1600 and 1750
Cantata	A musical work for a choir accompanied by an orchestra
Child prodigy	A young child who has an extraordinary ability, such as Mozart, who was able to conduct a professional piano recital at the age of 6 – something only an adult would usually be able to do
Classical	The musical period spanning the years between 1750 and 1830
Composer	A person who writes - or invents – pieces of music, like Beethoven
Composition	A piece of music written by a composer
Concerto	A piece of music written for a solo instrument and orchestra
Medieval	Music written before the year 1400
Movement	A section in a piece of music similar to a chapter in a book
Musical form	The structure, or type, of musical composition. For example, a concerto
Musical theme	The main melody in a piece of music. Usually the first melody you hear
Musicologist	An academic expert in musical composition
Opera	A musical play in which the words are sung

Opus Another term used to describe a musical piece or work

Orchestra A large group of musical instruments that play together with a conductor

Patron, A patron pays a musician so that they can carry out their work, much like a sponsor today.

Phrase A group of notes put together in a way that works like a sentence in a piece of writing. Together, the notes in a phrase make sense and can stand alone.

Recital A performance was given by a musician playing alone

Renaissance The musical period spanning the years between 1400 and 1600

Romantic The musical period spanning the years between 1830 and 1900

Score A piece of music in written form

Secular music Music that is not religious in nature

Sonata A piece of music in three or four parts, written for a solo piano or orchestral instrument with piano accompaniment

String quartet A group of four instruments with strings playing together

Symphony A long piece of music written for orchestra, usually with four movements

Index

R

S

T

V

W

Books in the Classical Giants Series:

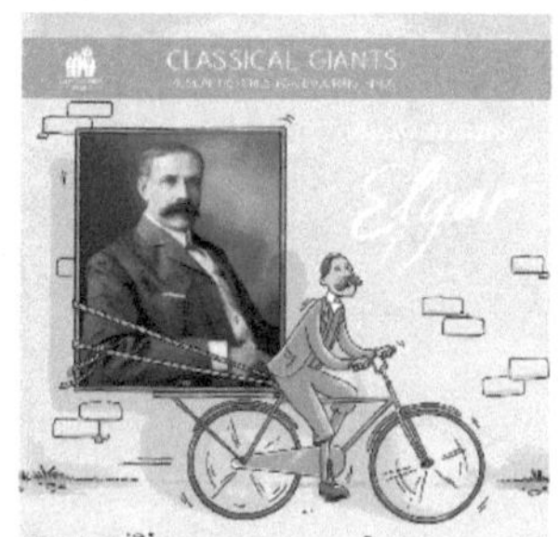

Which one will you read next?

www.classicalgiants.com

Illustrated by Evgeniia Lanskikh 😊

Made in United States
Troutdale, OR
10/19/2024